AF268905

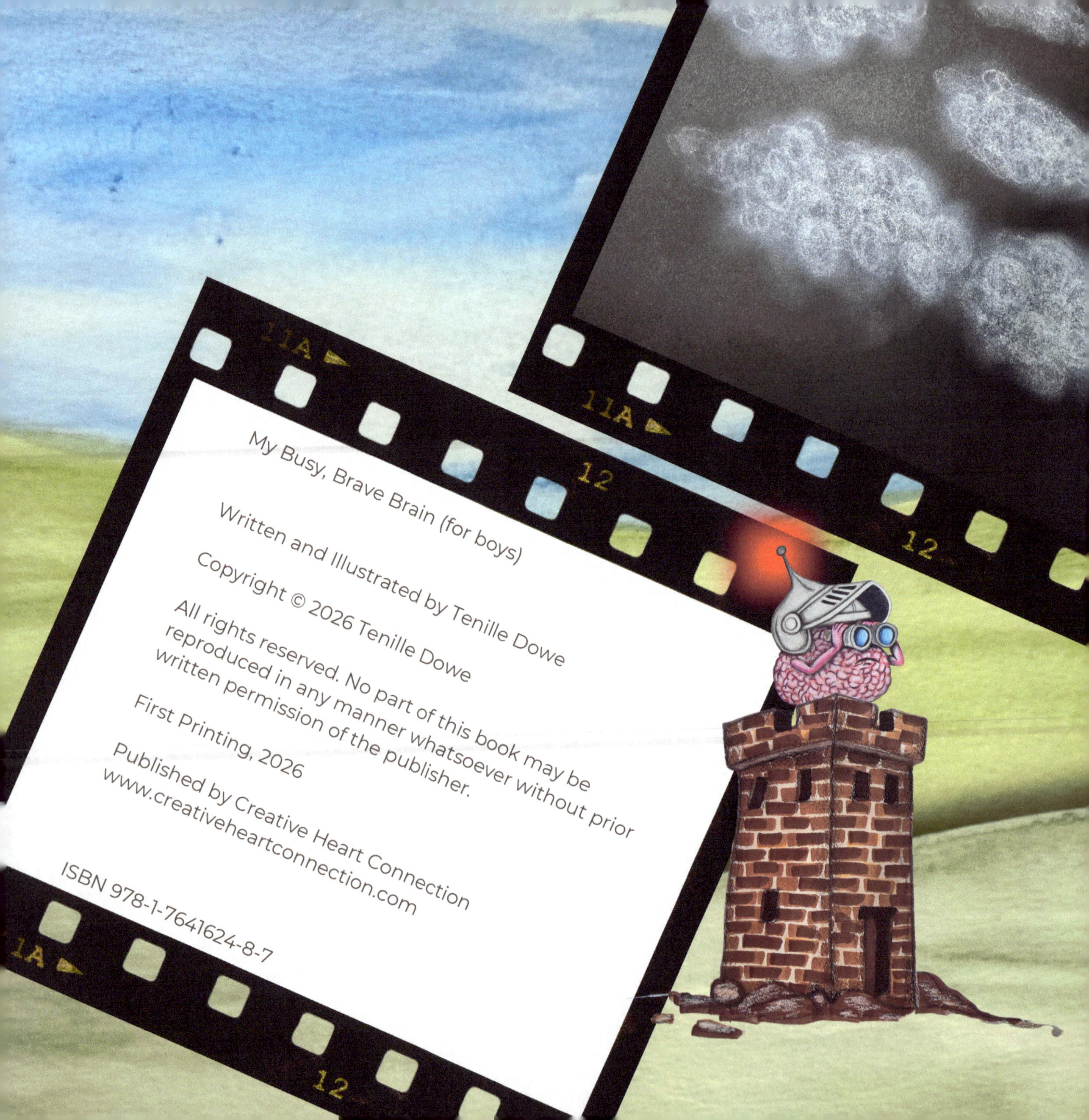

My Busy, Brave Brain (for boys)

Written and Illustrated by Tenille Dowe

First Printing, 2026

Published by Creative Heart Connection
www.creativeheartconnection.com

ISBN 978-1-7641624-8-7

My Busy, Brave Brain
Written and Illustrated
by Tenille Dowe

Everything looks calm... but my body feels different.

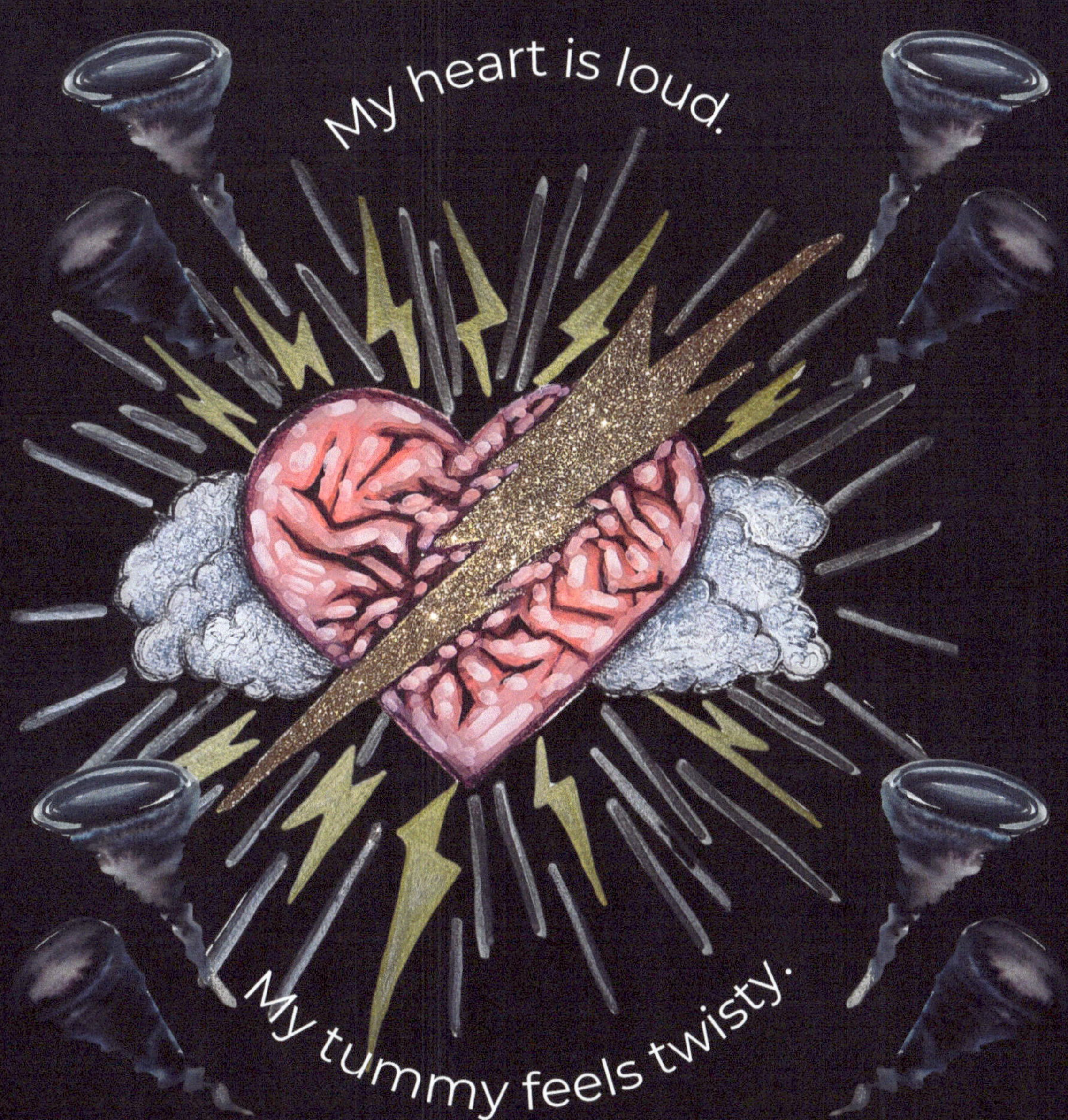

My heart is loud.
My tummy feels twisty.

High above, my busy,
brave brain is always watching.

"Storm warning," it whispers.

My body gets ready... just in case.

BANG
BOOM
CRASH
SHOCK

BOOM
BANG
CRACK
THUD

Nothing scary is happening...
but my body thinks it is.

My brain remembers storms from long ago.

It is trying to keep me safe.

Everything feels heavy.

My hands feel shaky and cold.

WHOOSH
WHOOSH
WHOOSH
When everything feels too much, my busy,
brave brain helps me float and fly through
fluffy clouds, giving me space to rest,
stay safe, and come back when I'm ready.

"You've been watching for a long time," I say.

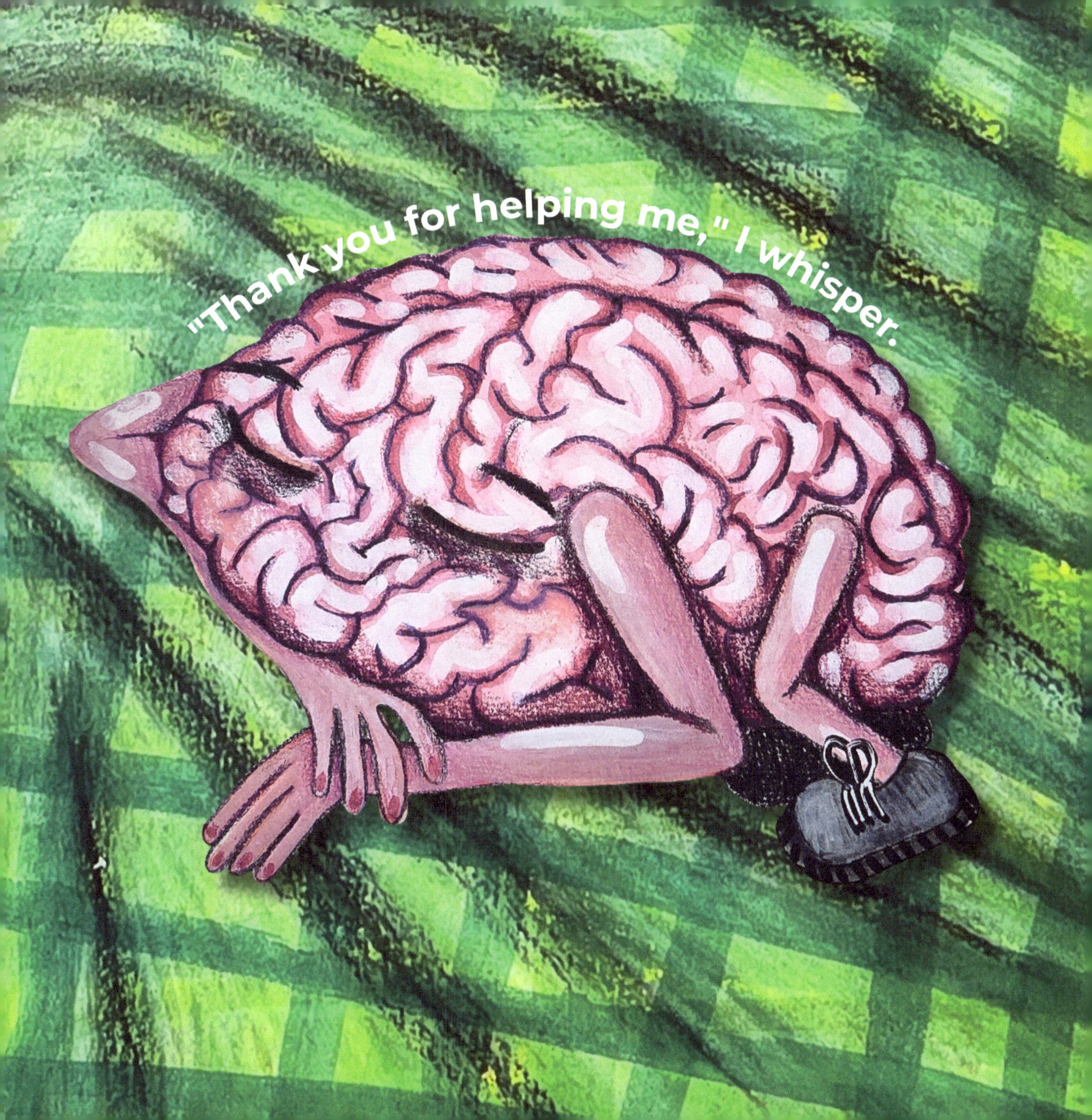
"Thank you for helping me," I whisper.